St. Franci

REV. JUDE WINKLER, OFM Conv.

Imprimi Potest: Michael Kolodziej, OFM Conv., Minister Provincial of St. Anthony of Padua Province (USA)
Nihil Obstat: Rev. Msgr. James M. Cafone, M.A., S.T.D., Censor Librorum
Imprimatur: ✠ **Most Rev. John J. Myers, J.C.D., D.D.**, Archbishop of Newark

The Nihil Obstat and Imprimatur are official declarations that a book or pamphlet is free of doctrinal or moral error. No implica-
tion is contained therein that those who have granted the Nihil Obstat and Imprimatur agree with the contents, opinions or state-
ments expressed.

Francis Is Born

WHEN one hears the name St. Francis, most people think of St. Francis of Assisi, but he was not the only St. Francis to come from Italy. There was another St. Francis, this one from the town of Paola in southern Italy, who sought humility above all things. He and his followers are called the Minims, a name taken from the Latin which means "the least." They wanted to be the least of the least, and yet he and his order had a great influence upon the Church and the world.

St. Francis of Paola was born in the part of Italy called Calabria in 1416. His father was named James and his mother Vienna. They were poor farmers who were not well educated, but they were wise in the ways of the Lord.

Their faith is especially seen in their devotion to St. Francis of Assisi. They had been married for many years and still they did not have any children. So they turned to their favorite Saint, Francis of Assisi. It was not long afterward, on March 27, 1416, that Vienna and James had their first child. They named their baby Francis in honor of St. Francis of Assisi, the Saint through whom they had received their great desire.

FRANCIS'S family was poor, as was almost everyone in that part of Italy. Because of this, they could not afford to give their son much education. He did live with the Franciscan friars for a year during which he learned to read.

And yet Francis's family taught him what was most important in life. They taught him to place God above everything else. For the rest of his life, he spent countless hours in front of the Cross, meditating on how much God loves us. He had a great devotion to the Sacrament of the Eucharist as well, never missing an opportunity to attend Mass. He also had a devotion to the Blessed Virgin Mary, praying the Rosary as he meditated on the Mysteries of our Faith.

Francis's family also took him on a number of pilgrimages to shrines throughout Italy. They took him to Rome and Assisi and a number of other places where his spiritual growth continued.

When he was only fifteen years old, Francis asked his parents for permission to live as a hermit. A hermit is someone who lives alone and spends many hours during the day and night praying.

The Beginning of an Order

ONE would not think that this type of lifestyle would draw many followers, but when he was nineteen years old two other young men joined Francis. At first they lived in a cave, but the local people were very impressed with their holy way of life, so they built them three small huts and a chapel. A parish priest would come to celebrate the Mass for these holy men each day.

Most religious orders, like the Franciscans or Dominicans, take three vows, promises to God to live the Gospel without property, in chastity, and in obedience. Francis added a fourth vow to these three. He promised to live a life of fasting. In those days, the fast during Lent was very serious. People would not eat meat, cheese, or eggs all through Lent. Francis and his followers promised to observe that fast all year long.

Francis did not make this promise because he hated the world. He did it because he wanted to devote himself entirely to the Lord. People sometimes misuse food, eating too much or too little or the wrong thing. They worry about what they are to eat or drink or wear. Francis remembered Jesus' instruction to be like the lilies of the field, trusting in God for everything.

The Founding of the Minims

THE number of those who wanted to live like Francis and his first two companions continued to grow. By 1452 there were enough of them to seek approval from the local Archbishop to become a religious order. He gave them his blessing. They were called "the Hermits of St. Francis of Assisi," but later on they changed their name to "the Order of Minims," the least brothers, meaning that they wanted to be the least important of all people.

Francis and his companions also built a new monastery for themselves as well as a new church for the many people who were beginning to visit them. The people of that region held them in such high esteem that they all helped them in their building project. It was most inspiring to see the rich working alongside the poor peasants as they built a house for God and His servants.

As the years went on, more and more people came to visit Francis and his followers. So many came, in fact, that the Holy Father, Pope Paul II, sent someone to check out this new group to make sure that they were faithful to the teachings of the Church. He found Francis laying stones for their new church building.

The Holy Father Gives His Approval

THE representative of Pope Paul II was so impressed with Francis that he reached out to kiss his hands. Francis pulled his hand back and said that it was he who should kiss his hands for he had celebrated Mass as a priest of God for thirty years. (In many countries people kiss priests' hands as a sign of respect.) This made it even clearer to the representative that Francis was a man of God, for no one had ever told Francis that he had been a priest for thirty years.

As much as he was impressed by Francis, he was not too sure about his way of life. He thought that eating no meat, cheese, or eggs all year long might make Francis and his followers sick.

At this point, Francis reached out into the fire and pulled out a handful of red hot coals. He held them in his hands for quite some time, and when he put them down and held up his hands to show the Pope's representative, there was absolutely nothing wrong with them. This convinced him that God was behind what Francis and his followers were doing.

In 1474 the Holy See officially approved of this new order.

Other Miracles

WHEN someone is as close to God as Francis tried to be, he often receives the power to perform miracles.

Once, while they were building the church near his monastery, the workers began to complain because of the long distance they had to travel to get water when they were thirsty. Francis struck a rock with a stick and water immediately began to flow out of it. This spring still produces water today.

Another time when he was traveling, his donkey needed to have new shoes. These shoes are nailed into the hoof of the animal to hold them in place (it doesn't hurt the animal). After the blacksmith finished putting the shoes in place, he asked to be paid for his work. Francis explained to the blacksmith that he didn't have any money. When Francis told the donkey to give back the shoes on its hoofs, the donkey stepped right out of them.

One of the most famous miracles is when he crossed the Straits of Messina from Italy to Sicily. He had no money to pay the boatman, so he took his mantle, laid it on the water, and floated across the Straits as if he were on the safest of boats.

The Power to Tell the Future

FRANCIS also showed his openness to the Holy Spirit when he was able to tell the future on a number of different occasions.

In 1480, he was able to foretell that the Turks who were Muslims were going to capture the city of Otranto in Italy. He also predicted that the king of Naples would soon capture the city back, and this is just what happened.

Another time he was speaking with the Holy Father. Up to this time, the Holy See had not yet approved for the Minims to fast all year long. The Holy Father told Francis that he was still not ready to do so. Francis told him that it was all right, and pointing to one of the Cardinals said that he would do so when he became Pope. That Cardinal became Pope Julius II, and he gave official approval for the year-long fast of the Minims.

During that same visit, a powerful man named Lorenzo de Medici told his seven-year-old son to "kiss the Saint's hands." Francis predicted, "I will become a Saint when he becomes the Pope." This young boy grew up and became Pope Leo X, the Pope who canonized Francis as a Saint in 1519.

An Invitation for the King of France

AROUND this time, King Louis XI fell ill. He was not a very nice man. He even had a nickname, "the spider king," because people thought he was sneaky and as dangerous as a spider.

The king heard about the holy man Francis through some merchants who had come from Naples (a city not far from where Francis lived). Louis was afraid to die and desperate to be cured. So he sent an invitation to Francis to travel to France to cure him. He promised Francis all sorts of rewards if he would do this, but Francis just ignored the invitation. He was not going to seek the very riches that he had rejected all of his life.

Louis had great influence over Ferdinand, the king of Naples. He had Ferdinand repeat the invitation, but Francis once again just ignored it.

Finally, Louis went to the Holy Father, Pope Sixtus IV. The king of France and the Pope were not really all that friendly, but the Pope realized that if he could get Francis to go to France, then Louis would owe him a favor. So Pope Sixtus IV ordered Francis to travel to France so that he could heal the king, and Francis obeyed.

A Triumphant Journey

WHEN Francis left his monastery in Paola, he bid farewell to his brothers. He knew in his heart that he would never return to his homeland.

The first part of the trip was made on foot and by donkey. Whenever he passed through a village, the people would gather around him, begging him for his blessing.

When he reached Naples, he received a magnificent welcome. The king of Naples and crowds of people treated this humble man as if he were a great king.

Then, when he reached Rome, he was invited to meet with the Pope and the Cardinals. The Holy Father was so impressed with Francis that he offered to ordain him as a priest, but Francis turned down this honor for he wanted to remain a simple hermit.

When Francis finally reached France, the welcome was even more incredible. The king rewarded the first man who brought him news of Francis's arrival with a gift of ten thousand pieces of gold. He sent his son to accompany him to the palace. When he arrived there, the king bowed down to him and kissed his hands.

Will the King Be Healed?

FRANCIS had been invited to France to heal the king. He proved that he could heal people all along the way, for he entered cities that were suffering the plague and healed those who were ill with a blessing. Would he heal the king?

The king visited the holy man almost every day, and he often asked him to heal him, but he didn't get an answer. Rather, Francis kept advising him how to be a better Christian and ruler. Finally, the king's patience wore out, and he openly asked Francis whether he would heal him or not.

Francis's answer surprised the king. Rather than receiving the answer that the holy man would heal him, the king heard that his life was drawing to a close and he should get his soul in order.

One would have expected the king to be angry and possibly send Francis back to Italy, but the king knew that this was truly a holy man. Everyone had seen how he spent long hours in prayer and ate only the simplest of foods. Even though Francis and his companions were dwelling in a palace, they were really living as simply as they had in their monastery. And so the king followed Francis's advice and prepared his soul to meet the Lord.

AFTER the king died, there was no lessening of Francis's importance. Because the new king was too young to rule on his own, his sister Princess Anne acted as his regent. (Regents are people who rule in the place of kings or queens when they are too young or ill to rule themselves.) She asked Francis to pray that she might have a child, and sometime later she gave birth to a daughter.

He also advised Charles, the new king, to marry a princess of Brittany. The two royal families of these lands had been fighting for a long time, and this marriage brought peace to their regions. Earlier he had brought peace to France and Spain when he advised King Louis XI of France to return some disputed territory to Spain.

Here was a simple, humble hermit, an uneducated man, who was giving advice to the royal families of Europe. He might have been uneducated according to the standards of the world, but he was wise according to the judgment of God.

Even people from the great University of Paris recognized his talents and sought his advice. This was also true of many members of religious orders.

All Things to All People

FRANCIS'S wisdom was especially seen in the way that he treated people. He did not treat them all the same way but in the way that he thought would be most useful for them to come to God. With some of them he was gentle and understanding, with others he was harsh as he condemned their evil deeds.

We see an example of him being gentle when he crossed the Straits of Messina on his cloak. At first he had asked a boatsman to carry him across, but the man had refused to do so unless he were paid. When the boatsman saw the miracle of his crossing on his cloak, he begged for forgiveness from Francis. The holy man readily forgave him.

It was also said that when he would return from a trip and he was told that one of his brothers had not been living up to his vows the way that he was supposed to, Francis was always ready to forgive him.

But he could also be quite harsh with people who deserved it. He disliked people who would tell lies to hurt others. He even condemned the rich and powerful when they abused people.

MUCH of Francis's spiritual advice is found in the many letters he wrote to his followers, to rulers, and to anyone who sought his advice.

To his followers he wrote, "My beloved sons, whom I love so much in Christ, I am already leaving you for France. I remind you first of all to love our merciful Father in Heaven, Whom you should love and serve with all your strength and purity of heart; secondly, I counsel mutual love. You shall mortify your body with a fruitful and reasonable penance, by which you will be freed from falling into the snares of the devil."

In another letter he advised, "Be peace loving. Peace is a precious treasure to be sought with great zeal."

He also wrote, "Take pains to avoid sharp words. Pardon one another so that later on you will not remember the injury."

He stated that our greatest source of spiritual strength is reflecting upon the sufferings and death of Jesus, "Fix your minds upon the Passion of our Lord Jesus Christ. Inflamed with love for us, He came down from heaven to redeem us."

The Spread of the Minims

EVEN though Francis and the Minims did not seek power or fame, their holiness brought them many friends and followers. Francis saw his order spread throughout southern Italy and Sicily.

When Francis came to France, the order began to spread there as well. Part of the expansion was due to Francis's influence in the royal court. Part of it was simply the people's recognition of how God was working through this humble hermit.

In the meantime, King Ferdinand of Spain received a piece of advice from Francis (that he should not let his troops retreat in a battle that they were fighting against the Moors). He followed that advice and quickly won a great victory. In gratitude, King Ferdinand invited Francis to establish the Order of Minims in Spain as well. From there, one of the Minims even accompanied Columbus on his second trip to the New World.

Meanwhile, the emperor of Austria invited the Minims to come. They opened three houses in his empire, two in southern Germany and one in Bohemia.

King Charles of France also helped the Minims to establish a church in Rome.

30

FRANCIS, in spite of his many penances, lived a long life. About three months before his death at ninety-one, he received a revelation from God that he would soon die. He spent the next three months alone so that he could dedicate himself totally to prayer and contemplation.

Then, on Palm Sunday, he developed a high fever. Even though he was weak, he wanted to attend all of the services during Passion Week to commemorate the Passion of our Lord.

On Holy Thursday, he attended the Holy Eucharist. Later, all of his brothers gathered together for a ceremony that is called the Chapter of Faults (during which they confess their sins and shortcomings to each other). Francis asked his brothers' forgiveness for when he might have been too strict with them. He hugged them and kissed each of them goodbye.

Then, on Good Friday, he asked someone to read the Passion from the Gospel of John. His last words were a prayer for good people and sinners, among whom he included himself. He then seemed to be staring at something glorious, and he went home to the Lord.

Francis, Saint and Patron

IT did not take long for Francis of Paola to be declared a Saint. He died on April 2 of 1507, and he was canonized by Pope Leo X only twelve years later. (Remember, this was the same person whom Francis had predicted would become a Pope and canonize him when he was only a boy of seven years old.) His feast day is April 2.

Many people have sought his intercession, and he has become the patron of sailors, of those suffering from epidemics, of travelers, and those seeking protection from fires. Many couples also pray for his intercession so that they might receive the same favor he had received for Princess Anne of France: a healthy child.